criss cross

p. inman

ROOF BOOKS
NEW YORK

ISBN: 0-937804-57-6
Library of Congress Catalog Card No.: 94-068498

Design by Deborah Thomas.
Back cover photograph by Quinn Robinson.

for Tina
& for Jack

Acknowledgements
"my drift" contains bits of pieces published in the *Roof* and *Brilliant Corners*
between 1977 and 1979. It's dedicated to Bruce Andrews. "stead" contains
language drifted from an uncollected portion of "Dust Bowl" published in
Verse. The author would like to thank Art Lange (*Brilliant Corners*), Jerome
McGann (guest editor, *Verse*), and James Sherry (*Roof*) for their encourage-
ment and support. "smaller" is an homage to the director Alain Resnais and,
in particular, his film "Mon Oncle d'Amerique". "Foxrock, near Dublin..."
refers to the birthplace of Samuel Beckett and is dedicated to same.

This book was made possible, in part, by a grant from the New York State
Council on the Arts and the National Endowment for the Arts.

Roof Books
are published by
Segue Foundation
303 East 8th Street
New York, New York 10009

criss cross

TABLE OF CONTENTS

lines contained to grist. tan hy-

"brim"

drox. the space between Califor-
nia above the jaw. the knock i left
nooned metis. her reach maned to
older women. the still pore of an
arm, prose arrived to fragments.
pulch. work stoppage balled up

as content. moeb grammar. neck
crossed out on the damage longer
than he could think. Giotto com-
pared to poured brow. the edges
rubbed off exactly upon her throat.
the pour of how they wall up

lamp glows from brick dust
jacket. cave nicotine gaze re-

moved. Calvin's loyalty to the
word & not the image. a horn
of film Comanche drake stretch
emptied from a page. the lake
of it thin people to dots. felt
vug. H-block Long Kesh. pay

rate in bird language think tan-
ning their slow. rows upon
pitch relations past striped in.
that point of time, thin from
small talk. ocean imagery with
lipstick. modicumed passenger

the passengers the exact french
to their knees. light spread out
by the time. the crossed out field

in her breath. the wool in a verb
now that it's over. lace eaux.
how can any square have makes.
the writers i prefer by one by
distance of Russian novels. an
anise of last minute. childhood

labor laws off the books again.
black hair without the time
scale to it. toffee logan. her
sing off his fingertips. cones
as lukes. a round childhood
brook as the leverage behind it

jobs spelled from distances.
blemish vades. his back to
the wall grouped out of book
side, its whited beer by.

stillness paired with tire speck.
sentences once the mind ceases
secco. rubbed up nature. an
empty carport while i waxed
into a hill. woman seen from
behind further from her Dutch.

the daybreak that's left after.
every wheat gress step by step
stoved out. toothpaste cattle.
image at ice cyst. one last ridge
from waist source. brogue stull.
Inca marks on a box to himself

an hour to read the further away
it seems. the dream part without
the dearth. Guinness Book of
kinds of emphasis. smallpox
middle period. cornered sugar

hear. suppose the Rhine farmed
on their bread. figurine vaux.
speed crossed out from her mind
among the cats, sound as an oleo
unlike. nez of sculpt. the glimpse
the voice subtracts. pieces of

bread made of edges. a lined face
riced still. who defends wealth
into door repair their steps thicked
from. earshot without the thinned
burks. neast. the underclass to
the dictionary. flusts on paper

the last Byzantine met by waves.
posture hundredths. someone's
voice as it equals mine. their
eyes as far as space. popcorn
likelihood. the land around Ma-
tisse's Woman in a Red Blouse

pesters to feather. what he saw
was Holland a bit on the side
flattened out of brown river. a
tequila with balled list steers.
that glimpse settled out. ledge
vull. graped think with specks.

she would have died of Plague
sanded to lipstick. Hemingway
under the ball from Rhode Island.
the wrong words his nose broke
at her. linguistics before the
ballpoint pen. "waxed rice".

"as narrow"

a side Gabin film.
what i write in has no end.
sounds slimmed to eyelid.

cloud cover veugle.
each anisette from.
where she looks.
without beyond.

such o'clock on glasses.
names of river left.
on mape nose.
itches compared in mice.
the pesk at a room.
beneath the biography.
who else in Herzog.
meant a glass coach.
had what she read left afar.
slacked ball.
earshot aleck.
hours to middle Irish.
its lecture back strain.
Rizzuto deal.
brink tick makes.
such etch coal weem.
the last shot where James.
Taylor says anything.

clock've gluss.
can't be such partedness.
a girl's neck thin from.
what i couldn't pronounce.
flowed polder.
a Pittston that changes.
their bare feet.
neak caplet.
corner nicotine.
of light turned off.

"otherwise is that forever." a fill of
sentences the ditch of what i mean."
"the wet hole in stubs." "a pinochle
as in neutrals." "what i hear together
beneath how i orient it." "the spinach
of a book the same only two of it."
"picture sime." "awarded grant for
pulling blinds fits of lessening."
"too cold to write about carrotin."
"simmon of baptists denominations
stuck to money." "people knock on
the door leaving so much noise."
"every of doubt words into distance."

"my drift"

"an ice think prosed as much as you
can." "thinking about who's the real
Jack Kerouac." "an off-ball his own
aging." "white bye popcorn done in
nylon." "Union take-back into some
other person." "a book that greatens
into some white shirt to loosen up
simile." "the rest of the taste to how
slow it goes." "whenever we come
to Wagner more portrait turned toward
things." "years ago i'm less nation
state to myself." "how until is that
needed to freckle." "leam listened

listened afoot." "safflower of any
seems to be description." "is the
name of it before it happens." "it's
supposed to take what it means."
"an average too white to make it
as sculpture." "speriff." "ago potato
who have a paper voice." "self pro-
portionately." "makes of pepper of
of the same year." "the fill out on
youth think off some necklace."
each time Paterson appears more
skin." "is largeness at work out
to the Great Lakes." "cake appease."

"another handsome attack about the parking lot." "more skin through experience." "hour after hour the tape no longer exists." "thartic of reach doesn't occupy." "where you live didn't make the dictionary." "a limber of ball a tar of hears." "being thin at the Cotton Club." "twenty-five by foot with what i heard." "coholicky." "no presence appeal." "any connection to a total." "now's the midnight i should have told to makes of doubt." "underoccurred white wallpaper." "workers on voice lubricants."

"the taffy on abstraction." "think of less village out of the fattening." "howatch collapse." "everybody's these languages totaller than thou." "letting the woman in nomenclature." "is descriptive the matter that i have opium doubt." "an Inca Younger Poet." "hacker's license in red ink the length of a football field." "the lay down on content sugaring the insane." "epastic." "you determine it before it happens around on everything." "dying ain't much of a way to make a living." "the whole distance as much from speaking about it."

"stead"

the stillness smallest
after its stir. where does
nature stop (nothing fits
around palsy (the French
(dictionary quickly anymore.
thinking of her scar as
some number (all of the
of books. (Susquehanna
husband on urd (olfact
cigar plants shut down (in
world's largest (where
variety of bleach behind
reductio. (an applesauce
"Graham bread." (of her
the snub nose (one step.
beyond proverb (literacy

-

eight cents a (requirem.
meal sentence by sent-
ence (television about
(the color of leaves.

the same skin (the chimney
beer glass (she tallows
overlooking (through.
a meadow. "brown snow"
(how deep the world
supposing than avg. (might
Dick Powell (peruv. bygone.
the more he steaded
(life pissed away in talk.
handedness instincts.
bad walls denominator.

police riot (could be
at Flint (the prose left.
accent cleaner (each
sided daughter worried
about waves. (polka
normalcy a song be-
fore (chesapeake.
arithmetic (distinction
within the odd Baptist
(Neruda would write
"ven squad". (each
tannery (page beyond
inch settle (the page.
minuteh. (planet sauk
each vess enough.
an avereage (women
Hanover (in than.
40,000 words of
THE YEARS (list-
written in (erine
the shape of domesticated
animals (auburn w/.

hutterite each speakl.
lapped Catskill (speech
streamed in. (in looking
polka dotting (Mex.
the forecasted parts.
("wheat prices" their
speag (white before
applause side (celled
minutes not (Paulist.
quite right (the lean of
(her sing against theirs.
stacks of black chapter
starting at (statistical
(semitism. divided
French studies (into
billboard (pulse classes.
twenty percent of
his face is eyelash

iced itches. (the skull
how many (of a cow
sentences could (to
they miss in (set up
their head (another beer.

painter's neap. (the sun
undertow (light as it
about property (slows
(apart (thin of paper
Gorky poisoned (build.
about ceiling fixtures.
orch (pinto beans from
array (medieval days
river to. (backwards.
names of sight kinds
left in (how can any
(murder of Sandino?
shot of homeless (lean
    child five hundred
periods after (by vulp.

population privilege.
a deem (capital decline
hidden about (skin
glasses (opener, hear
Harlow's (around them
in its row (of mennonite.
Gide got politics (the
as he stopped (more
writing (night than
(land to her earring.
the forest as all (the
their voice. (soda up
"ouvrierist". (its brook

a last saucer (leap
upside down (month
Robert (from the mark.
Johnson beyond pro-
verb until 1936. (her
fraction (real name fro-
makeup vire (zen for
(the sake of publication.
persus o'clock peer
in. drink- (person
ing sterno (next to where
behind the beat (the
lined (nature stops.
eyesight built through

her eyelid (rices on
but periods. (where winter.
politics left from a
middle distance. (the
(rue lymph of how it
unknown how (distorts.
her mind is hummed
aside (shoplifted teeth
someone filled (marks.
with cheap cells (its
a pane of (oyster pro-
glass build (nouncing
outside them. (emphasis
Stein years after her
prose continued.(dulge
her build (phone cor-
glean wrong (ners
blood in miniscule.
black frost (idiom mice
company houses. (another.

staring man (the minutes
can't get out (around
of the sequence (him
in front of him (difficult
strews of mines (letter
how i gaze (flusts in.

a coal weem (the
could be (middle fraser
Monet as boundless. (of
jointed anomaly (a matter.
ended o'clock of fay
to it. (newt slum.
rices on a page (lost talk
memphis (by talk.
each to their appease

mice view (each graze
in plaid blankets. (the
lipst. (prose left in.

far name from ("long"
its mount aleck (as a plus.

skin of road (gist
either rustle (betweens.
her swim from pen stroke.
someone enlarged (side-
beneath the (walk
elongation (fester. a child's
(look in another pair.
foreign oil (candaced
without beyond (addi-
in Mexico. (tive. farm
climate as four (charp
cents a day. (mulberried
where the (about sculpture
working class (length
ranked in the land-
scape (of eyesight
(two years too late.
brown bird corpsed
but (a purblind
for punctuation marks

snow of folded hands.
staids as (fluence earp.
her apart eye (undertow
gone through (about
each trend (property.
some peck by their lights
(mind in her extent.

"passos fixity." (first
nucif. (glance as Montauk
on each zero. (taken away.
farming as pathology.
crinked o'clock. (pine casp
eightball of lake (enough
names (by tawned mind.
in the instant that i (settle
preached (as dark nez.

production relations (out-
(lasted lank. (male thatch
drink as a write within.
all of my nose (kinds of
put to book (brushwork
whatever (short. lell.
literature (punches to
beginning to shut (furn-
cattled scar. (iture parts
my nerves about (tan
train flattened (slended
on a white iotum (fr. wall

the bulk of his hat (a
& the room (round impasto
under it to (Geronimo.
an apple. (that memphis
he might (a white innate.
have seen the (whichever
person the last (slake it
wideness was to (looked
her. (upon. a song before
furred erase (compare.

drinking a scotch on
its side. (molecules of
Rothstein (social fabric
before some (to each
footage expanse (wide-
(ness his mind was on.
Andalusia com- (light
posed across a woman.
(source acreage. nerve
sitting (condition height.
at Ford plants (popcorn
prohibited. (done in.
the lime Montauk on
it by my lights. (rear
the last sound (fielder's
that lipst. (mitt in the
the same exact (time
speech from his (zone.
father's estate (deci-
the (mal kelve spread.
peopled lanolins to (black
a free drink (lung dowler.
cardboard barn (ocean

to Lot's wife. (rice
my name (behind gesture
as crayon arithmetic.
hunger printer's ink.
or the rehab (each blount
client from a button.
sight leather (of noun.
geneal. (each whose eyes.
than trombone drugstore

the dawn (had she paused
from its terms (enough
brist of (arm in. an aspirin's
revolution. (tanned since.
the longer the Ohio (book
(cattled out. could be sub-
however she (tract than
arrives frosted to. (fiction.
dusked sweat drops

everywhere's (pea crop
lecture side. (through
spearmint (such (ballgame
mow (words. (stachio.
painting problematic

"felicidade"

Fletcher Henderson with none of the credit budged through.
the haunch of what i mean the blunted fess to a crow. laned
money. my compared croft of her. the more wall the minusses
at some of its content (flinch ponded from). the gleam something
passes by as saunts. plove vertence. how i think the white
behind parents the lapse shape from me. remains wedded to

swim stroke. whatever earshot the mind has left. light neg

my walk stodge. a man in Indiana under the skin. light of a
kind but for the scratches he existed to (the middle name of a
mistake). the beeline as i resemble. outset strokes. their gleam
from brown river. itches under paper. ball sluff. the legs of
miners toward periods the bounds of a coal drake happen-

stance. narrowed wine put aside to the gesture. "the knobs on
things" a blunt of limit. their smallnesses put into writing.

echoed blunds. vuoy. its marigold tass. women with-
out objectifying them (the same entirety out of acts).

time seemed where she drove her car on the french.
lost cattle pieces where i can't. i was at letters too
straight to read. the same comment on Strindberg some-
what later. surface as resistance i missed for my chin.
each painter between her hodged eyes. benched wall

the less i was whited through time. some midst before
that inch. one's attention & the bristles it contains to
beat. nuss. a man loves his wife named after. another
prose that his glimpse has settled has another background
to depend on. lake oil customers. all the workmen left
at their footprints (the sauk along a line). "what inter-
ests me in Wales" is where to stand. laced tick bite

windows in Trenton from a speck. his trace pecked of
these figures first look turned to posture. cent brunt
eyesight slimmed upon it. in touch with work to put
the meaning aside the wider i grasp about Villon. the

lateness to a paragraph some blond of brim. set up eye-
lid Irish. time that goes by to become much earlier as
each graze tessed in lines. each odd from the mineral

bird combined from its other letter. for the renaissance

light was extent the same twenty people thinned to an
idea. piss road cells. the cattled skin of my shape. sun-
light after subtraction notion puffed on. termed starling.
snowstorm backdrop. the feeling of span the less i was
born. carpenter postures. hours than names of parted
creek. toothpaste with less. the blunt of some period

plotted lap. the tawn stell everything that her pulse. flap
cells on the back of my hand. the Charles R. with facts
around it. whited through time. pawed vore. where your

son resembles you past his mechanism. finched talk level.
entire border in a Cadillac to another northward point.
sifts of foothill a small jaw into door compounds that've
snowed off. a paragraph as long as i can last through it

"land's end"

such a thin of the book the beginning of an offspring beside
one line. how did distance become as dim as nosed. the brook
of edges in a dictionary. the shorten of her earrings. her least
voice land on. how much energy could be back from Austria.
talk based still. meiged prairie. the smoother peer he couldn't

the need his eyes closed the better. snowfall predictions &
my gums. how would the space empty the same buildings in.
the pattering which some light put out. some stretch it seemed
to part from. the light in the driveway into that much lap

he'd want the Hudson known past prose. shed ball tanned
extent in. flow lost in musses. the tawn pond of some
weight loss cloud cover across. posture tessed to listens.
flapped pen parts. a neap of bleeds the more beautiful.
where does snow fall by all the pronoun shapes. its piece-
work lapped from a pencil. cetera drape. each hour puffed
in to contain myself. suppose his footsteps stayed behind
his eye. black rice persip. where was she in her midst. my
nose hairs at the side of a wineglass steadying toward some
barn. what if what leaned from them could disappear from
with the same within the line of her knees from the parting
pages. bread lurline. the space between the trees & the hand-
edness on. the lines of the Shannon to a paragraph. fold
duz. finch of mesa. whatever had happened pulled down

a porcupine description into its smallest parts. each aside
where she has sunglasses. pissed fluorides. some bug itch
on a glass. "where did he get Colgate" the more the shape
is devoid of how i look. the germanism left from each shim-
mer of handedness. a look paused to black cattle specks.
pencil evers. one of Charcot's "staged observations". is he
thinking about beats or further off. my knee as their only
brim. nerved tracking shots. Beethoven's third period up
to whatever it's called. some tufts perioded from. the room

where the paint left off chinned into his desk. how the math
might happen coal strike as far build. she can't contain where
she's calved to literature. a map of wider space against a hat

where does her brink as thin rainfall. money leaned into
women as Black Hill dots. the world is around her not in
front. the facts are mussed with someone. shoelace brac.
widthed brook. a wineglass from the bottom glance of

how smart i am. each behind that my nedge eye. its same
avenue dutch. where did the back of her go prim of white
left after. his nose earshot leaned flat. car motor spunk

the short while that a landscape sulfurs to. nor the
road that my arm limes to a hatband. frontal or no.
B-cell firth. sided pinball stare pour buried. every
thought that has to end somewhere as tacks of stretch.
dictee lymph. king's men filled up against pen name.
each midst balled thin. such a calculative mode is
what opens up the space of things compared than
purblind. the flatness about lacking meters. a sleep
round but landed. pulse scrapes. what if the imagery
didn't dominate the song but merely became the

same rawbone pause her steps toward. black crack-
er spread. the line of her knees wooded to a ball.
"painting class because of Wagner." a tacked pinch

the dawn from terms sulfured to mice. no late could appear
that much chocolate. the trace of their modicums as some
chunk of box. spoken Inca to swim at. Berkshires on a field
from some wall. frankfurter spelling. he put the gray stripe
down the more that he underlined. her cheekbones through
some town. & the creased ice of that wait its hodge past adds.
stuck words on what she could see that far off. stricks of

ends. his fidgets from some put out light. brained tass of bank
teller. grape object crops. vactor. pen lengths crane beneath.
anise decimal. should i be looking at the intervals instead.
or the midst in their likeness. her peers landed from a page

the woods slimmed a while where his suit comes out.
a polk of the leverage there. a grain of lighting recall
grown to thin. the least stirring put down in writing.
padded light bathrobe "outfielders allowed". herd sun-
ders on which one stands. how would space cave my

eye under an inch. the taupe of a pin. ranked accent
marks. wherever i see someplace put into it. fixture
spots. bits of how i imagined the others met with facts

whose likeness from equal marks. the end of the page thin
craning in. the number of notes his lapses had alike. cheop
sidewalk. she meant more knee action tipped apart at the pale.
her statement always at that point before. back jay swim.
some actors as blocked story line balled earth on my lap.
the same idea but timed less. the brooked leam of her glance.
reased ice. someone shorter from here to what i'm doing.
nor an apple outset maned blank. trove farm flight. some

dot lean with desert parishioner's side earred under. stull
ovaltine. pen strokes on a waiting train. legged de camp

smallness reduced to footsteps. Pascal's blood problems in

a room the more hours toed of a mane. my nerves about inch
skills. mounded bellhop the men her age that were under a
moose. gulf edged in her lap. geometry veined from the states
on. padded dots. where does she remember about content & its
grape dusk. the rice French it means. clock prickles. all that
mist in her lap delled in say-so. pauses as boundary thins

"seche"

daybreak in its blonded tracks. an earth drake snow thins. his
room faced an overnightbag of large print emphasis a
tan dusk of pinches. where would the upper class tip over
into some page the blunt of them cried even. sweating the
wine out in memories. black lung bop crop with the width
through it. brinked feet. could a man describe a woman as

she missed through. italian sentences as optical mistakes

earred dashes. a man's arms to sifts sime bygone. slaked
under brains. what she imagines to snowfall compared off.
nerved blacktop. stelve boeuf. penmanship by 35 lipstick

canned into. elbow from the bottom background. how a
widow might be endless about her glasses field without
outset. lurge. verbiage tanned into lap. mining town vealed
about a snake. peers of tass black tack happens. glister

a terned ink. a nosed dot where culture each color of acreage. each pyrenee semblance. legged pen strokes from hats. saying grace before the dinner as the river widens vinegar at them. sight metis. her ear at its anacin tess. a single lasted woman. "men on roof" alike their pulses. punches to furniture parts. whosever sight the weather might compare to everything before she could control it. lymph output broken. scratched nose stilled of light

how any situation could come before them their peer slowed
to gist. the wrong pen how i flatten my midst to a drink. each
cake inkness behind eye. lesson passage. added up barndoor
cell from the previous lines words always at that point before.
the pause once the emphasis is left. neural teal than i can think

of. a mown sugar Rhine from the posture on it. sensation than
signification. Beowulf on the paper more nightfall but vast

small wavelets out to something. "every crime in Oklahoma"
heard to midsts. grape stroke production. the thought of her
footsteps shaped into hills. popol statistician. velm landscape.
are they the same thing varied slightly or different things anew

idea by parted bulldoze. checker ice of how i look. Black Hills
exactly alike. background stellate. people compared as initial-
isms. punched-in snowstorm. wall of bookshelves across my lap

how they think the distance left. a black liquid elapse. pine
bit lawn chair. my bone structure at a period. the longer some

knee stilled apart word for sound. homed speck. counts
holding meaning together via pieced cattle. holding a beer
his own height is behind. Scandinavians in Wisconsin their
every crissed etch. the city of Augsburg to the liver. sime
output scrapes. whosever sight nodged of hale. replica burks

the last eight stills in Mon oncle d'Amerique itched through
a rue lymph in long term the snub nose of a tomb from my chair
would the point be to disperse one's body that there are phrases
her comment on Strindberg down the driveway toward their car
the land where i think blurred on my eyes my neck sulfured short
artists work on their own adjustments in order to consider drinks
some sentences on how wide they are from the sunlight at tax time
watching while Monk couldn't name anything apart in Norwich
she was all the bygone passed through as some midst that its prim
there must be the least paper where i left it to that blank suitcase
that much longevity where she'd missed what he'd described to dot
had what she read left people stilled upon behind the wrong beat
John Dee's handwriting my glasses compared than egg-shaped
what couldn't be pronounced to its thinnest partedness of winter
how do notes fall from their light as the thin from its wedlock

"smaller"

a unit of length before she could remember her chin
"the closer we get to the building the less as we see"
what wouldn't be linked to the stretch aside from it
nerve tissue to fauvists as he reads about partedness
are the Amish their imaginations compared in mice
had she paused enough that i'd already spoken of
every painter from her eyes on literature to the stull
my neck to a point the time that it took me to write
my arms granted where my son asleep missed to dot
Catholic left on glasses from a pause from a chair
class position slimmed on how the later Beethoven
a pinstripe glean of French dictionary edge toward it
chapel intervals of all the collection the behavior left

her picture that never varied much ankle
how would i go past the world at a time
my nose in everything as acreage color
a girl's neck thin from where it named
a wheat soto as swim from pen stroke
sentences on how wide they are past
Colem. Hawkins more totally a distance
all the wrong wall from a bookmark
sunders into footsteps i never seemed
french river in her lungs to be normal
some clock on how he matters attention

Asian word calved periods on
carlights in a book on some hide
the cherokee a banker's grist
schedule texture on a waist
hours within trees of literature
the peer in my neck to a point
cow glance maned into birthr.
hutterite in some grape dusk
seeing cut off from some jots

nerve tissue to fauvists
ea. breath at my blunt
compound nabsico pts.
experience as interupt
a vint as french river
time & reproach study
Curtis Faville alikeds

stroud of hairc.
a nerved dutter
sunburn vaux
start meg dystr.
tucked minuteh.

loire culp
plove th'k
edge orv.

oipl.

"Foxrock, near Dublin..."

each gentle as the ditch is deep. the down of a landscape
onwards. description without morals iced to his or her
face. people i read about their spread hair showing through.
a glass of wine into three distances. the creek whiten
from an inside. nothing more out of so little

how is a first sentence ever past its blanch. the hill before
on more dimension as he thinks about dividing into dates.
the glean left where a woman's neck would outlast. had
she paused enough a small swim before. listen symptoms.
poor lighting destruction even as he couldn't put his
hand back to the car. shoreline pulver. what a landscape
means as he forgets

how many times could things be around her. a shale wane
a draught pith. the even part of her path who else streamed
in. row upon graze snowed mind off. earth increase perched
in. what he writes in has no end. the whole family where
he sat the thick of his final compare. my name sunburned
from a murmur

"after"

the bounds gone from.
their past. valvoline birdcall.
the line of her knees.
folded to days in dots.
lake budge. finched itch.
each weem snowed of him
might go once its oddness.
a childhood the entire.
inch of her swim.
a page of plot-line
boundaried under. veff.
where to stand background.
hunters from Wisconsin.
her name sketched through.
the smallness inside.
mind's tassed grasp.
portraiture all pissed out.
capsize dicter furthest at-bat.
why my arm matters.
to some of the content.
he put the gray stripe down.
the more he darked behind.
"grammar with" where.
ever one really left.
beer differs made of kinches.
staired lace fess.

"hackensack"

the less a small group of Shak-
ers crops amounted to them. a
woman's knees so that the pict-
ure can end. the inned absence
to a person. what i need nerved
in more bird. frosted warpath.

the written blunt out of every-
thing. my shoe & what it counts
for. simply a war between the
classes surviving before their
name. peopled brill sleep tall-
owed off them. whomever might

be seen the longer the cattle re-
semble. how any situation by
its structure surrounds my mouth
lasts. based service entrance, eye-
horn at the same dime. her eye-
sight as it remained landscape

is that where he imagines the
movie stops a ball to elds. birch
nerve. phrase of wedlock weight
training with handouts. whatever
de Kooning made temperature
slowed to dots. my nerves a

single woman surrounded on a
checker. the even bread that the
sunburn represents. not in the
mind formed around. thin stops
of bone structure. earshot with-
out graze. all the longevity my

swim divided before. had
one paused enough into bulk.
stooped bites. the red hair of
who i am. sidedness as stone
dot. their ink stime of nose

every period as the blunt to a
ball. haze of arm composed of
crow attention. kined wood
cells. brime of haircut. one
might be noosed of length &
all that under the nerves they

had of us. each one's sing lined
gnaw. the Tennessean in a name
alone. oddball steach. woods
skinned of slow consumption. a
great body of water of slender mel-
odist. the long haul about pose

in his work. a luke of pesters.
mineralled stomach-ache sepa-
ration on paper stopped that long.
decimal tess. the cease furred of

hunger snowed of her. the An-
des in red trees. as much fore-
arm as they leaned on the light.
iodide catcall. the tass of some
spine. the exact swim of what
i'd described. paper composed

to mice. lank spots. whatever
one looks at closed up with earth
the French on the three of them.
my shadow & the cattled scar
it takes. an ash stelm of mind
ball. the front of my eyes left

under time. ice weem. age landed
on bare trees. their stead after.
the brink on her every swim.

propaganda filled with gull.

blanched saxophone. some periods
through the wall. she can't contain
where she's calved gaze. a single
woman ponded to quotes. owner-
ship of the coal but not the coal.
timber sift of dark poppies. train

speck made of traits. coast sulp.
the beige of prose i lost. a body
some woods shaped into rock.
brown class counts. how can i
write some pause on, Black Hills
poached around the eyes. a point

as lasted as her height, creek
draped in. the vim to the soda

two centuries long the longer her
waves resemble nouns. nostril
damage on a pin. Harry Bridges

shaped from squirrel word ever
lieu. his palsy coaled from. the
finched piece to be dead. a shine
parlor behind bird part. is that
where he imagines the movie
stops. as everything left after sub-

traction. the noun amounts thinned
off in a car. its scot entirety. its
slant from workmen. i'm where
the land wears out to nothing sur-
rounded on a tire. short equals my
knees mazed on. statement lepsy.

everywhere rounded from my past

OTHER ROOF BOOKS

Andrews, Bruce. **Getting Ready To Have Been Frightened**. 116p. $7.50.

Andrews, Bruce. **R & B**. 32p. $2.50.

Bee, Susan [Laufer]. **The Occurrence of Tune**, text by Charles Bernstein. 9 plates, 24p. $6.

Benson, Steve. **Blue Book**. Copub. with The Figures. 250p. $12.50

Bernstein, Charles. **Controlling Interests**. 88p. $6.

Bernstein, Charles. **Islets/Irritations**. 112p. $9.95.

Bernstein, Charles (editor). **The Politics of Poetic Form**. 246p. $12.95; cloth $21.95.

Brossard, Nicole. **Picture Theory**. 188p. $11.95.

Child, Abigail. **From Solids**. 30p. $3.

Davies, Alan. **Active 24 Hours**. 100p. $5.

Davies, Alan. **Signage**. 184p. $11.

Davies, Alan. **Rave**. 64p. $7.95.

Day, Jean. **A Young Recruit**. 58p. $6.

Dickenson, George-Thérèse. **Transducing**. 175p. $7.50.

Di Palma, Ray. **Raik**. 100p. $9.95.

Dreyer, Lynne. **The White Museum**. 80p. $6.

Edwards, Ken. **Good Science**. 80p. $9.95.

Eigner, Larry. **Areas Lights Heights**. 182p. $12, $22 (cloth).

Estrin, Jerry. **Rome, A Mobile Home.** Copub. with The Figures, O Books, Potes & Poets. 88p. $9.95.

Gizzi, Michael. **Continental Harmonies**. 92p. $8.95.

Gottlieb, Michael. **Ninety-Six Tears**. 88p. $5.

Grenier, Robert. **A Day at the Beach**. 80p. $6.

Hills, Henry. **Making Money**. 72p. $7.50. VHS videotape $24.95. Book & tape $29.95.

Hunt, Erica. **Local History**. 80 p. $9.95.

Inman, P. **Red Shift**. 64p. $6.

Inman, P. **Criss Cross**. 64p. $7.95

Lazer, Hank. **Doublespace**. 192 p. $12.

Legend. Collaboration by Andrews, Bernstein, DiPalma, McCaffery, and Silliman.
  Copub. with L=A=N=G=U=A=G=E. 250p. $12.

Mac Low, Jackson. **Representative Works: 1938–1985**. 360p. $12.95, $18.95 (cloth).

Mac Low, Jackson. **Twenties**. 112p. $8.95.

McCaffery, Steve. **North of Intention**. 240p. $12.95.

Moriarty, Laura. **Rondeaux**. 107p. $8.

Neilson, Melanie. **Civil Noir**. 96p. $8.95.

Pearson, Ted. **Planetary Gear**. 72p. $8.95.

Perelman, Bob. **Face Value**. 72p. $6.

Perelman, Bob. **Virtual Reality**. 80p. $9.95.

Piombino, Nick, **The Boundary of Blur**. 128p. $13.95

Robinson, Kit. **Balance Sheet**. 112 p. $9.95.

Robinson, Kit. **Ice Cubes**. 96p. $6.

Scalapino, Leslie. **Objects in the Terrifying Tense Longing from Taking Place**. 88p. $9.95.

Seaton, Peter. **The Son Master**. 64p. $4.

Sherry, James. **Popular Fiction**. 84p. $6.

Silliman, Ron. **The New Sentence**. 200p. $10.

Silliman, Ron. **N/O**. 112p. $10.95

Templeton, Fiona. **YOU—The City**. 150p. $11.95.

Ward, Diane. **Relation**. 64p. $7.50.

Watten, Barrett. **Progress**. 122p. $7.50.

Weiner, Hannah. **Little Books/Indians**. 92p. $4.

For ordering write:

SEGUE FOUNDATION, ROOF BOOKS, 303 East 8th Street, New York, NY 10009